THE TRUTH ABOUT DRAGONS

BY THOMAS KINGSLEY TROUPE

ILLUSTRATED BY JEFF EBBELER

PICTURE WINDOW BOOKS

a capstone imprint

Thanks to our advisers for their expertise, research, and advice:

Elizabeth Tucker, Ph.D., Professor of English
Binghamton University, Binghamton, New York

Terry Flaherty, Ph.D., Professor of English
Minnesota State University, Mankato

Editors: Shelly Lyons and Jennifer Besel
Designer: Lori Bye
Art Director: Nathan Gassman
Production Specialist: Jane Klenk
The illustrations in this book were created with acrylics and ink.

Picture Window Books
151 Good Counsel Drive
P.O. Box 669
Mankato, MN 56002-0669
877-845-8392
www.picturewindowbooks.com

Printed in the United States of America in North Mankato, Minnesota.
092009
005618CGS10

All books published by Picture Window Books
are manufactured with paper containing at least
10 percent post-consumer waste.

Library of Congress Cataloging-in-Publication Data
Troupe, Thomas Kingsley.
The truth about dragons / written by Thomas Kingsley Troupe,
illustrated by Jeff Ebbeler.
p. cm. — (Fairy-tale superstars)
Includes index.
ISBN 978-1-4048-5745-2 (library binding)
1. Dragons—Juvenile literature. I. Ebbeler, Jeffrey. II. Title.
GR830.D7.T76 2010
398'.469—dc22
                                        2009030399

Here Be Dragons!

Stories tell of dragons that are big and scary. But are dragons real? Of course not! Dragons are make-believe characters in fairy tales.

History of Dragons

Tales of dragons come from many different places around the world. The oldest tales started in Europe and China. The stories tell us there are different kinds of dragons.

Where do dragons come from? In many stories, dragons hatch from large eggs, much like birds.

According to the stories, dragons live a long time. A dragon isn't old until it lives more than 1,000 years! Plus, dragons get stronger and more powerful with age.

What Do Dragons Look Like?

Storybook dragons often look like huge dinosaurs. They have scales all over their bodies for protection. A dragon can also have horns on its head. It has large, colorful eyes. Spikes line its giant tail.

Dragons come in many colors. Some are even shiny, like metal.

European Dragon

large leg

wing

scale

Dragons in European stories have large legs and mighty wings on their backs. Most dragons have four legs. But some have even more. A dragon's wings don't have feathers. Instead, the wings look like a bat's wings.

Dragons in Chinese tales look more like snakes. They have smaller legs than European dragons. Chinese dragons don't have wings, but that doesn't mean they can't fly. With magic, the Chinese dragon soars through the sky!

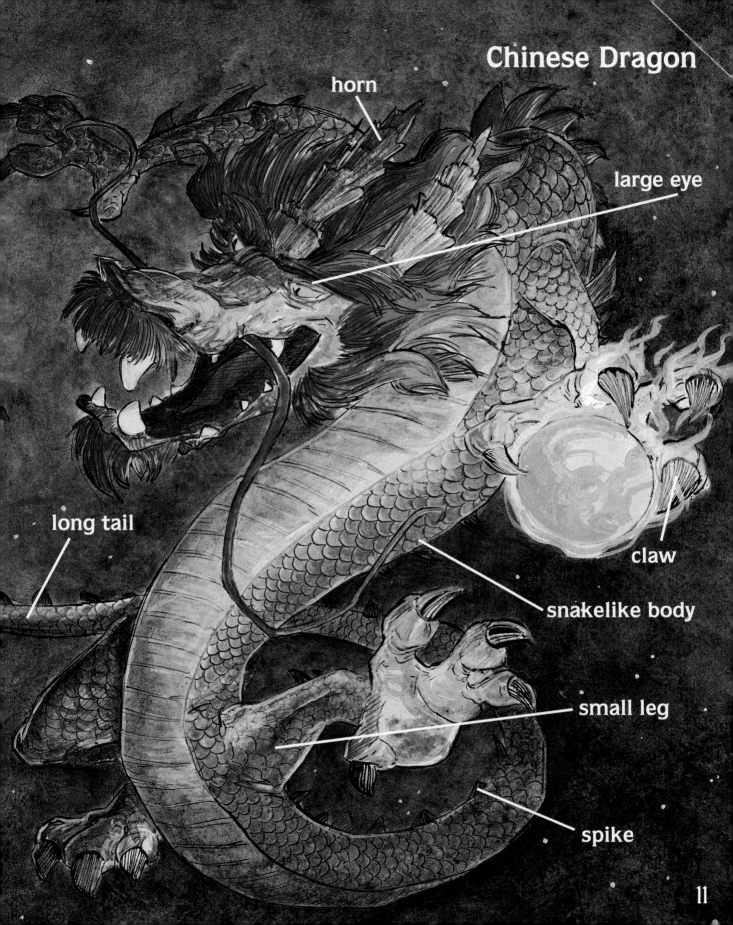

Chinese Dragon

horn

large eye

long tail

claw

snakelike body

small leg

spike

Where Do Dragons Live?

Like most make-believe creatures, dragons live in hidden places. A dragon's home is called a lair. Most dragons live in large caves that are hard to find. Caves help keep dragons hidden from enemies.

Some dragons choose castles for their lairs. First, dragons scare the people away. Then they settle in.

Legends claim that most dragons are cold-blooded. A dragon must find a way to warm itself. The inside of a volcano is the warmest place for a dragon to live. Hot rocks can heat up even the coldest dragon.

Dragons love treasure. A dragon needs a lair large enough to store its gold and jewels. Once a dragon finds a place to live, it usually stays there. Moving all its riches would be too big a job!

Dragon Behavior

In almost all stories, dragons are smart but scary. They attack anything that comes near their lairs.

Most dragons can breathe fire. With a mighty roar, a dragon blows a big blanket of flames. Dragon fire can burn villages, forests, and anything in its path. Some dragons can even spit fireballs. If you see smoke coming out of a dragon's nostrils, look out!

Other stories tell of dragons that spit acid. Some dragons freeze their enemies with ice, or put them to sleep with a poisonous gas.

Dragons also attack with their giant tails. A dragon's tail can smash houses to bits. It can knock over trees or make the ground rumble.

Not all dragons are evil creatures. In some stories, they are friendly and wise. Sometimes they can speak human languages. Because they live for so long, dragons know a lot about the world.

Dragon Tales

In many fairy tales, evil dragons kidnap princesses, destroy towns, and steal treasure.

The Deerhurst Dragon is a short tale about a terrible dragon. In the story, the dragon eats farm animals and ruins a village. A farmer leaves gallons of milk for the dragon to drink. A full belly of milk makes the dragon fall asleep. The mighty beast is then destroyed.

Knights are often sent out to fight dragons. *Saint George and the Dragon* is a famous story. In it, a princess is about to be eaten by a dragon. The king promises all his riches to anyone who will save her.

A knight named Saint George rides near the dragon's lair. The dragon appears. Saint George fights and quickly wins the battle against the dragon. He saves the princess.

Dragon Watch

In more recent books and cartoons, dragons are friendly to children. *Puff the Magic Dragon* is a poem written in 1959 about a dragon that becomes a boy's best friend. The poem became a song and later a cartoon and a picture book.

Dragons Today

Dragons are more popular than ever. Dragons appear in today's stories and in many other places. Dragons show up in movies, books, and even as sports team mascots. Many people see these make-believe creatures as symbols of luck and courage.

Whether fierce or friendly, dragons are real only in our imaginations. Still, it's fun watch the sky to see if dragons are among the clouds!

Fun Facts About Dragons

- Dragons don't shed their scales. As they get older, their scales grow on top of each other. That makes their skin very tough.

- Most dragons can swim. They move their tails back and forth to move quickly through the water.

- No one is sure why dragons like treasure so much. It may be that the treasure attracts brave (and tasty) people to their lair!

- On old maps where land was unexplored, some mapmakers drew dragons and the words *Here Be Dragons*.

- Dragons don't like seeing themselves in mirrors.

- A baby dragon is called a wyrm (WORM).

- Dragons live alone. If two dragons are together, they're usually fighting!

Glossary

acid—a liquid that can burn or eat away at things it touches

cold-blooded—having a body temperature that changes with the animal's surroundings

knight—a soldier from long ago

lair—a dragon's home

scales—small pieces of tough skin that cover a dragon's body

volcano—a mountain or hill that has a vent from which lava, rock, and hot gases are thrown into the air

Index

To Learn More

More Books to Read

Pringle, Laurence. *Imagine a Dragon*. Honesdale, Penn.: Boyds Mill Press, 2008.

Wang, Ping. *The Dragon Emperor: A Chinese Folktale*. Minneapolis: Millbrook Press, 2008.

Wiesner, David, and Kim Kahng. *The Loathsome Dragon*. New York: Clarion Books, 2005.

Yarrow, Peter, and Lenny Lipton. *Puff, the Magic Dragon*. New York: Sterling Pub., 2007.

Internet Sites

FactHound offers a safe, fun way to find Internet sites related to this book. All of the sites on FactHound have been researched by our staff.

Here's all you do:

Visit *www.facthound.com*

FactHound will fetch the best sites for you!

Look for all of the books in the Fairy Tale Superstars series:

The Truth About Dragons
The Truth About Fairies

The Truth About Princesses
The Truth About Trolls